More Professional Tools

EMT'S TOOLS

ANDERS HANSON

Consulting Editor, Diane Craig, M.A./Reading Specialist

A Division of ABDO
ABDO
Publishing Company

visit us at www.abdopublishing.com

Published by ABDO Publishing Company, a division of ABDO, P.O. Box 398166, Minneapolis, Minnesota 55439.

Printed in the United States of America,
North Mankato, Minnesota
102013
012014

Editor: Liz Salzmann
Content Developer: Nancy Tuminelly
Photo Credits: Shutterstock

Library of Congress Cataloging-in-Publication Data

Hanson, Anders.
EMT's tools / Anders Hanson ; consulting editor, Diane Craig, M.A./reading specialist.
pages cm. -- (More professional tools)
Audience: Age 5-10.
ISBN 978-1-62403-072-7
1. Emergency medical technicians--Juvenile literature. 2. Emergency medical services--Juvenile literature. I. Title. II. Title: Emergency medical technician's tools.
RA645.5.H362 2014
362.18--dc23
2013022504

Super SandCastle™ books are created by a team of professional educators, reading specialists, and content developers around five essential components—phonemic awareness, phonics, vocabulary, text comprehension, and fluency—to assist young readers as they develop reading skills and strategies and increase their general knowledge. All books are written, reviewed, and leveled for guided reading, early reading intervention, and Accelerated Reader® programs for use in shared, guided, and independent reading and writing activities to support a balanced approach to literacy instruction.

CONTENTS

MEET AN EMT!

WHAT DOES EMT STAND FOR?

EMT stands for "**emergency medical technician.**"

WHAT DOES AN EMT DO?

EMTs go where someone has been badly **injured.** They start treating the person right there. Then they bring the person to a hospital.

WHY DO EMTs NEED TOOLS?

Tools help EMTs treat patients before they get to hospitals.

EMT TOOLS

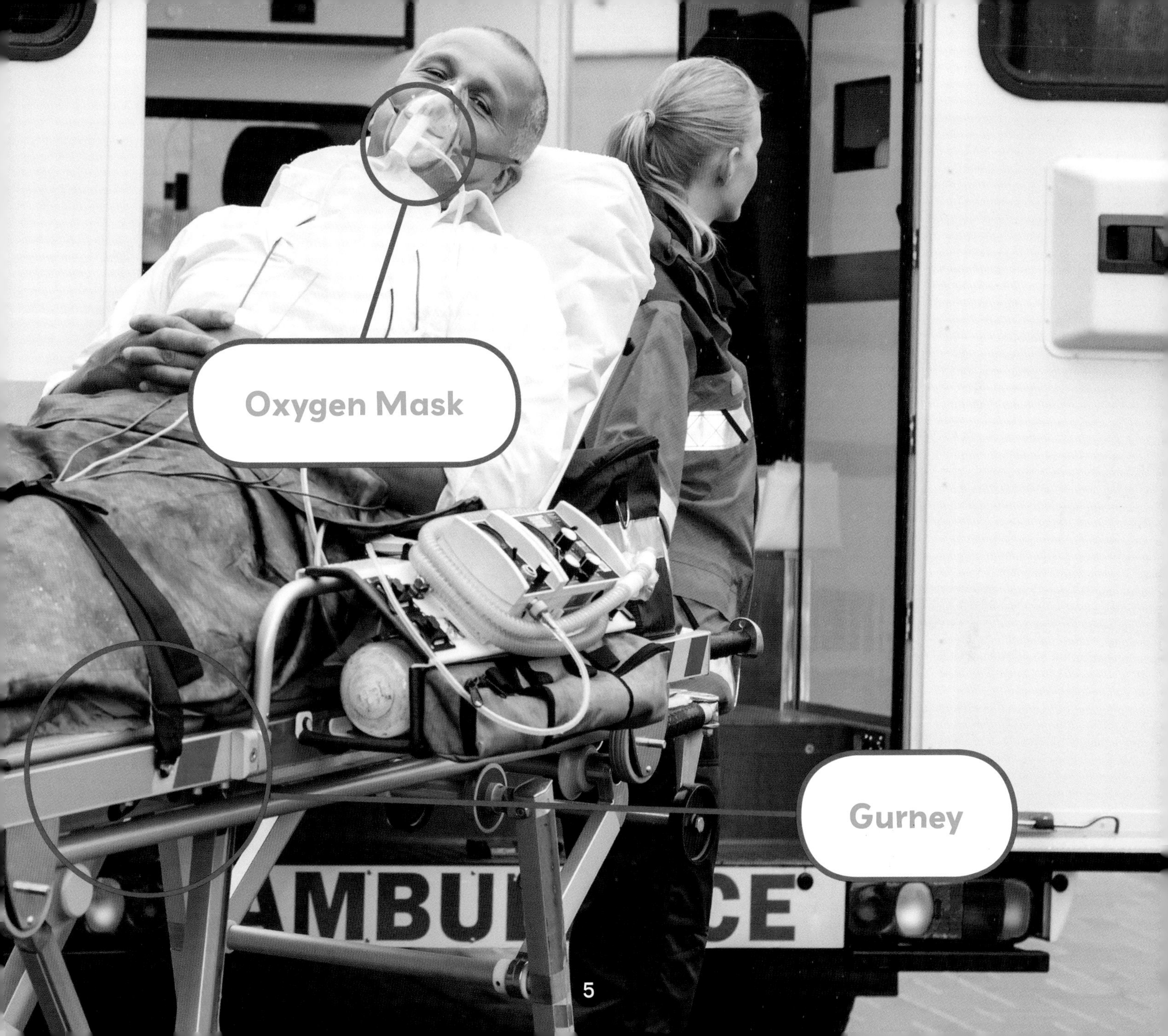
Oxygen Mask
Gurney
AMBU
CE

AMBULANCE

Ambulances are like hospitals on wheels.

Ambulances carry EMTs and **medical equipment.**

EMTs need to get to **injured** people quickly. To get there faster, EMTs turn on **sirens** and flashing lights. They tell other drivers to get out of the way.

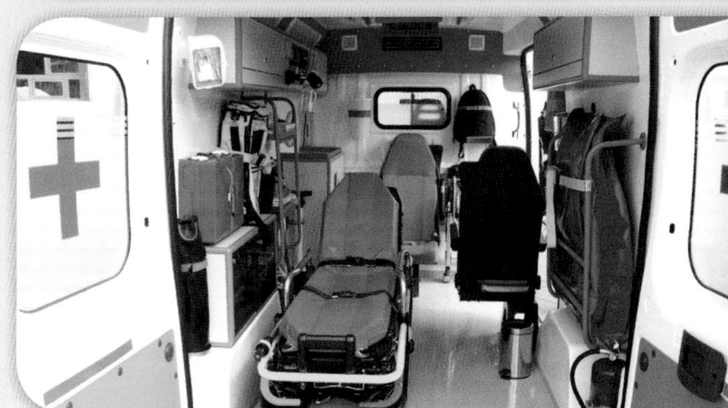

FAST FACT: Early ambulances removed **injured** soldiers from **battlefields.**

Paula and Claire are EMTs. Paula drives the ambulance. Claire helps direct her to the scene of an accident.

FAST FACT: During the 1970s, regular cars were converted into ambulances.

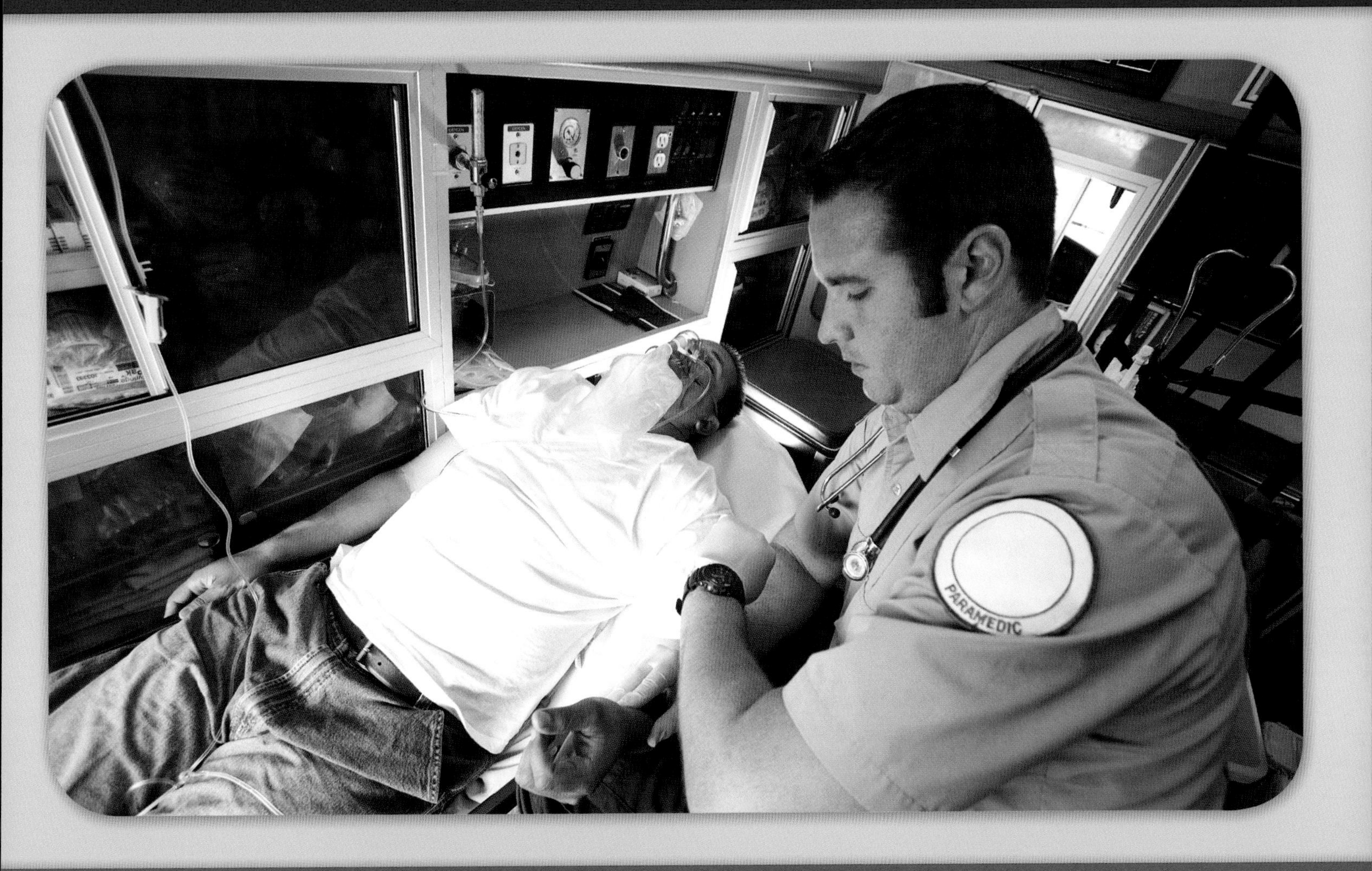

Bill is an EMT. He is trained to treat patients. He takes a patient's pulse.

DEFIBRILLATOR

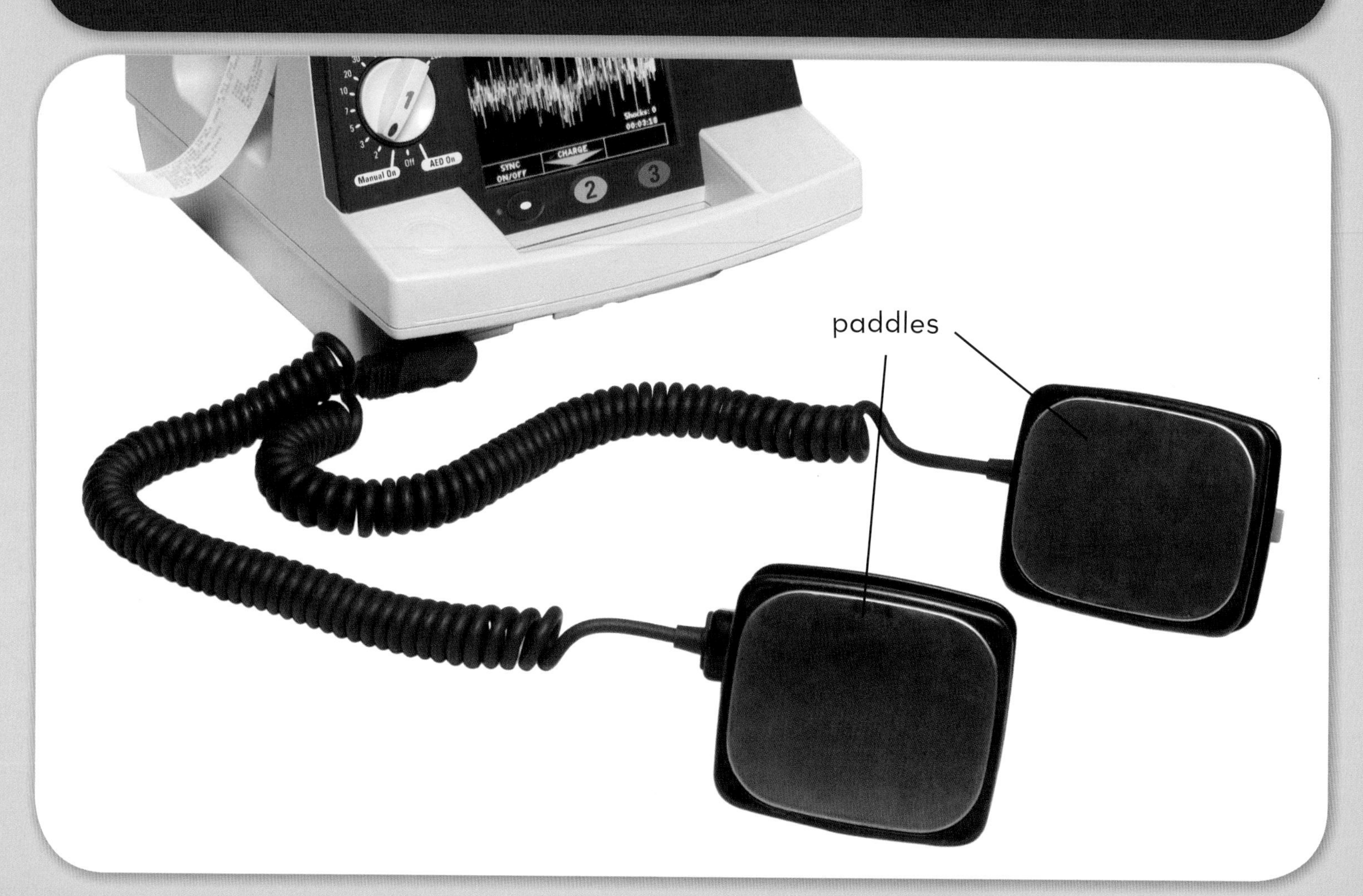

Defibrillators can restart a stopped heart.

A defibrillator uses an electric shock to restart a heart. Each defibrillator has two paddles. The paddles are charged with electricity. They are placed on either side of the heart.

When the EMT presses a button, the electricity goes into the heart. If the heart is healthy enough, it will start beating again!

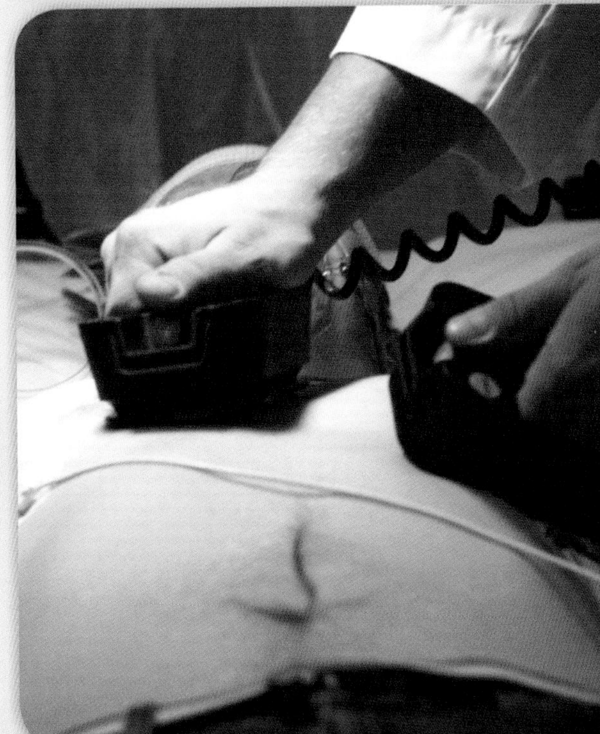

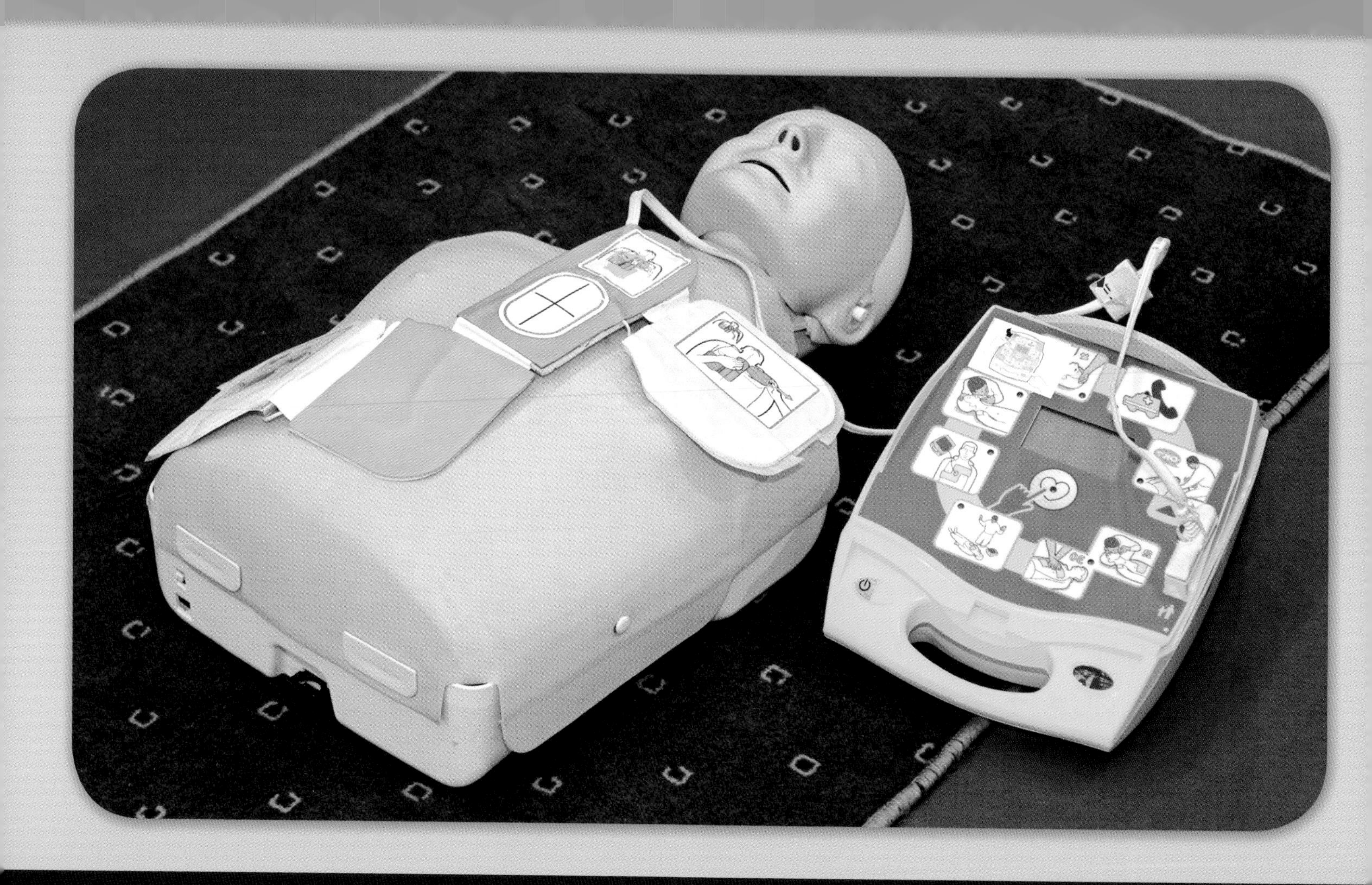

EMTs are trained to use defibrillators. They practice the correct way to use one on dummies.

FAST FACT: EMTs use **portable** defibrillators. They can be used anywhere.

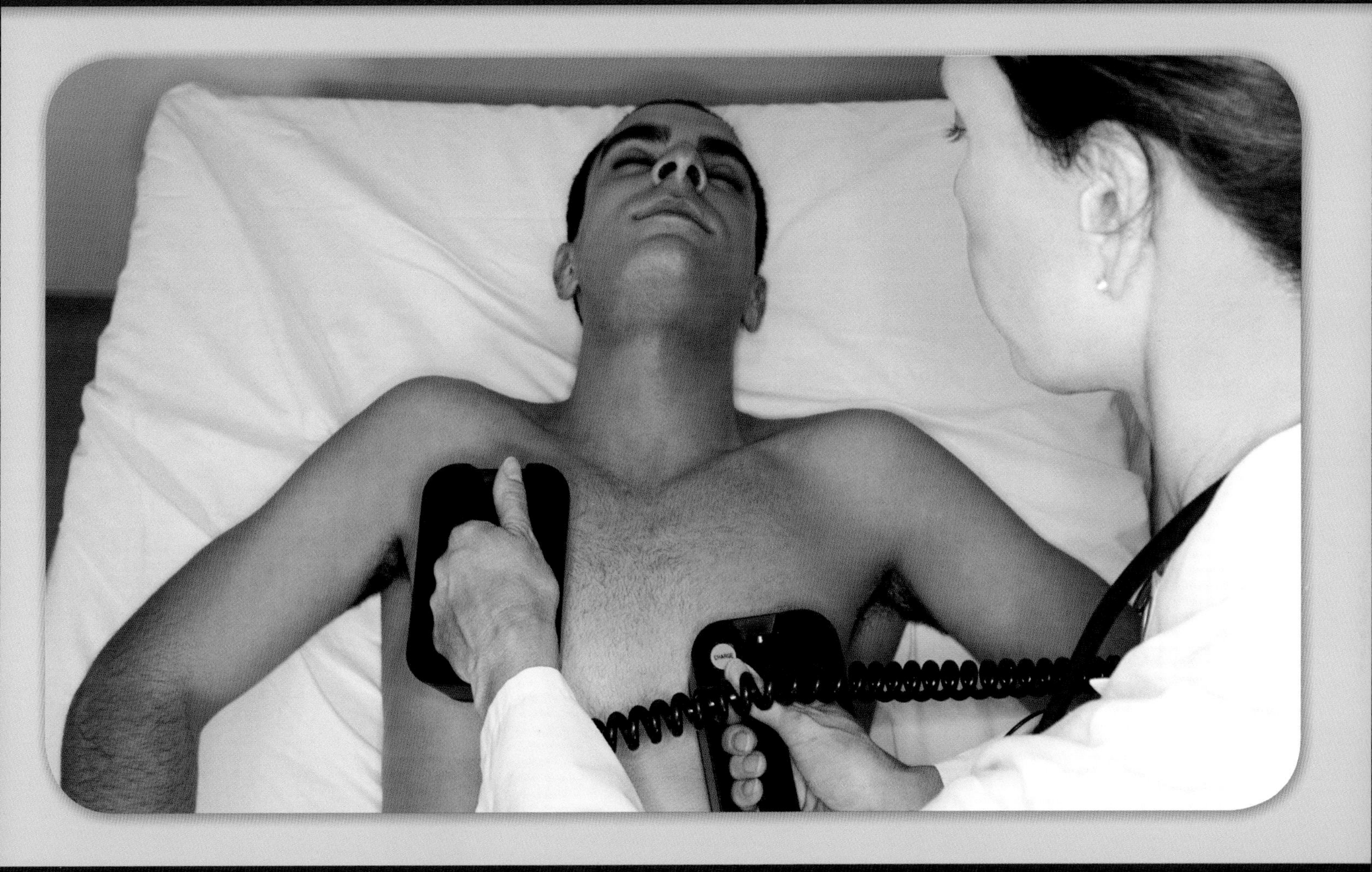

Jason's heart has stopped. Alexa tries to revive him with a defibrillator.

GURNEY

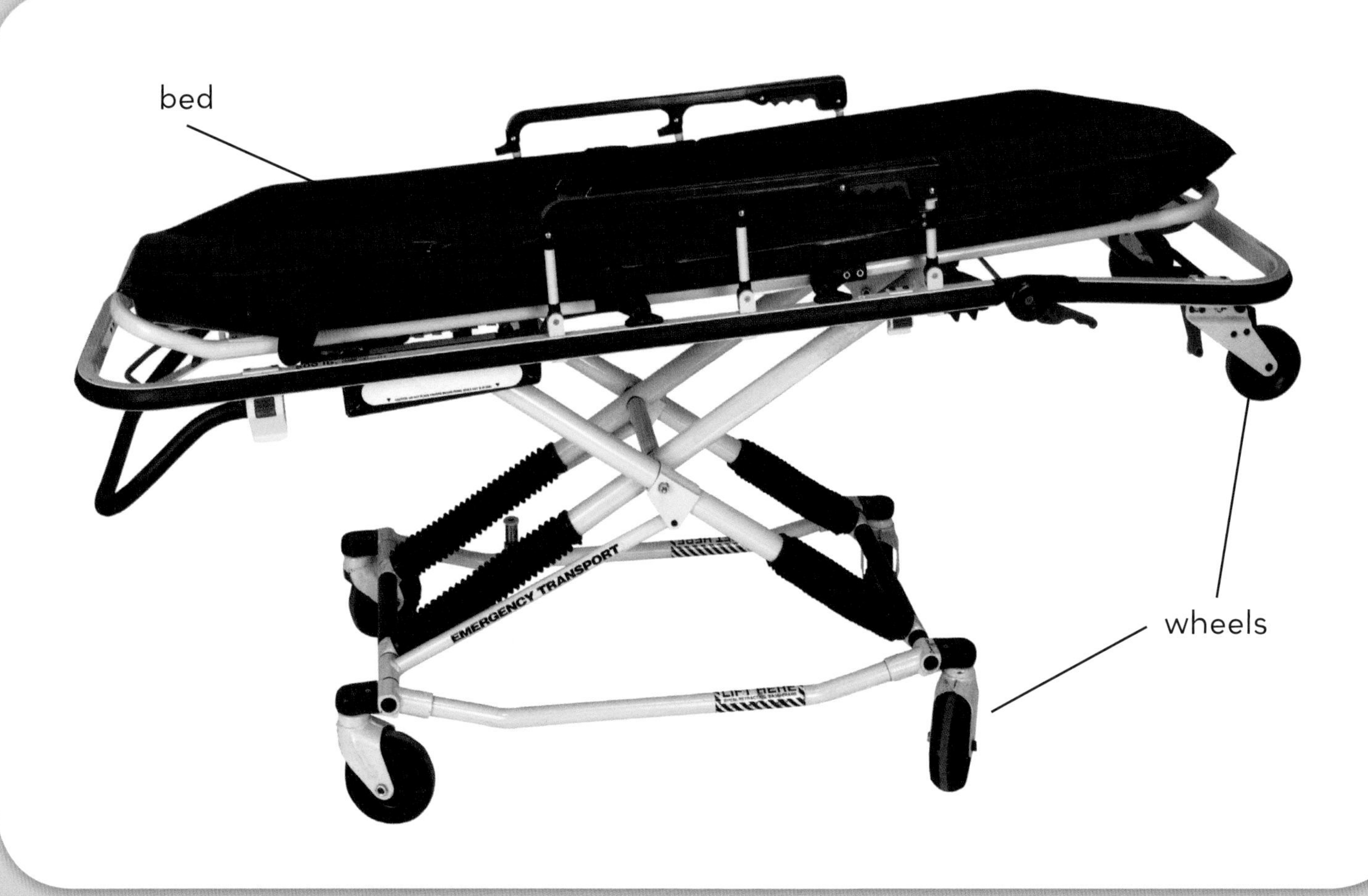

Gurneys move injured people.

A gurney is a bed with wheels. **Injured** people are placed on the bed. The wheels allow EMTs to move the gurney easily.

There are gurneys on most ambulances. The gurney lets EMTs carefully move patients to and from the ambulance. When the gurney is put inside the ambulance, its wheels fold up.

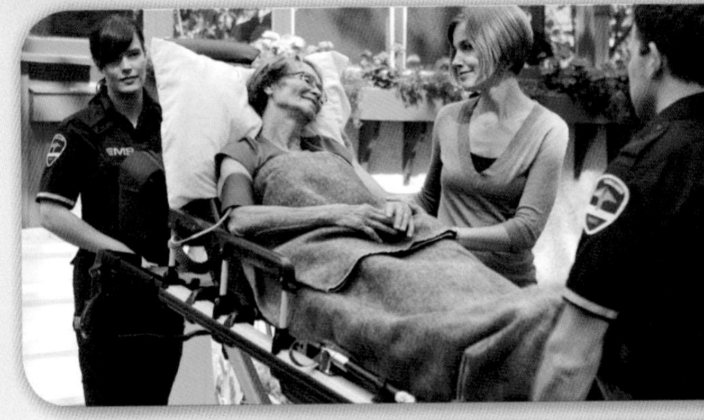

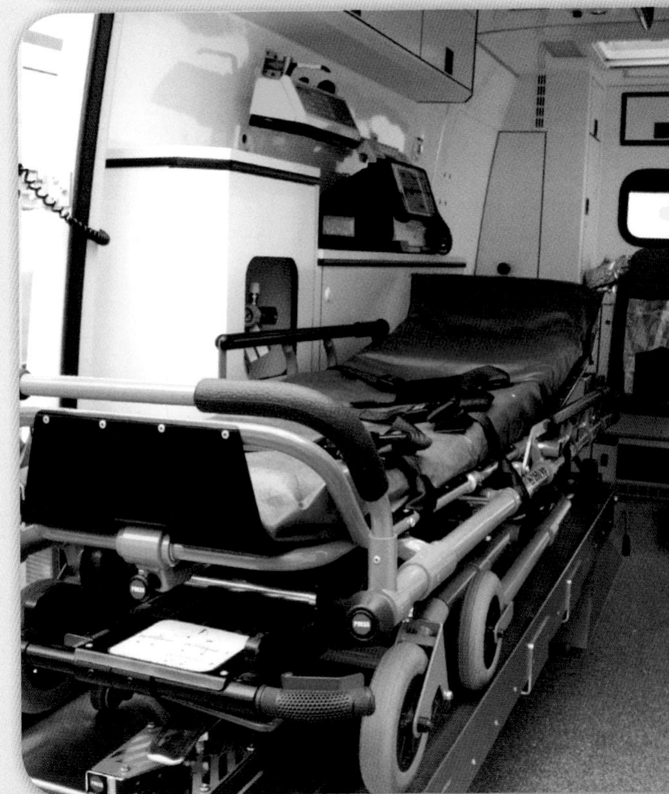

FAST FACT: Gurneys are similar to **stretchers.** But stretchers don't have wheels.

Frank and Jennie help move a gurney. They are taking a woman to the hospital.

FAST FACT: A gurney's bed can be raised and lowered.

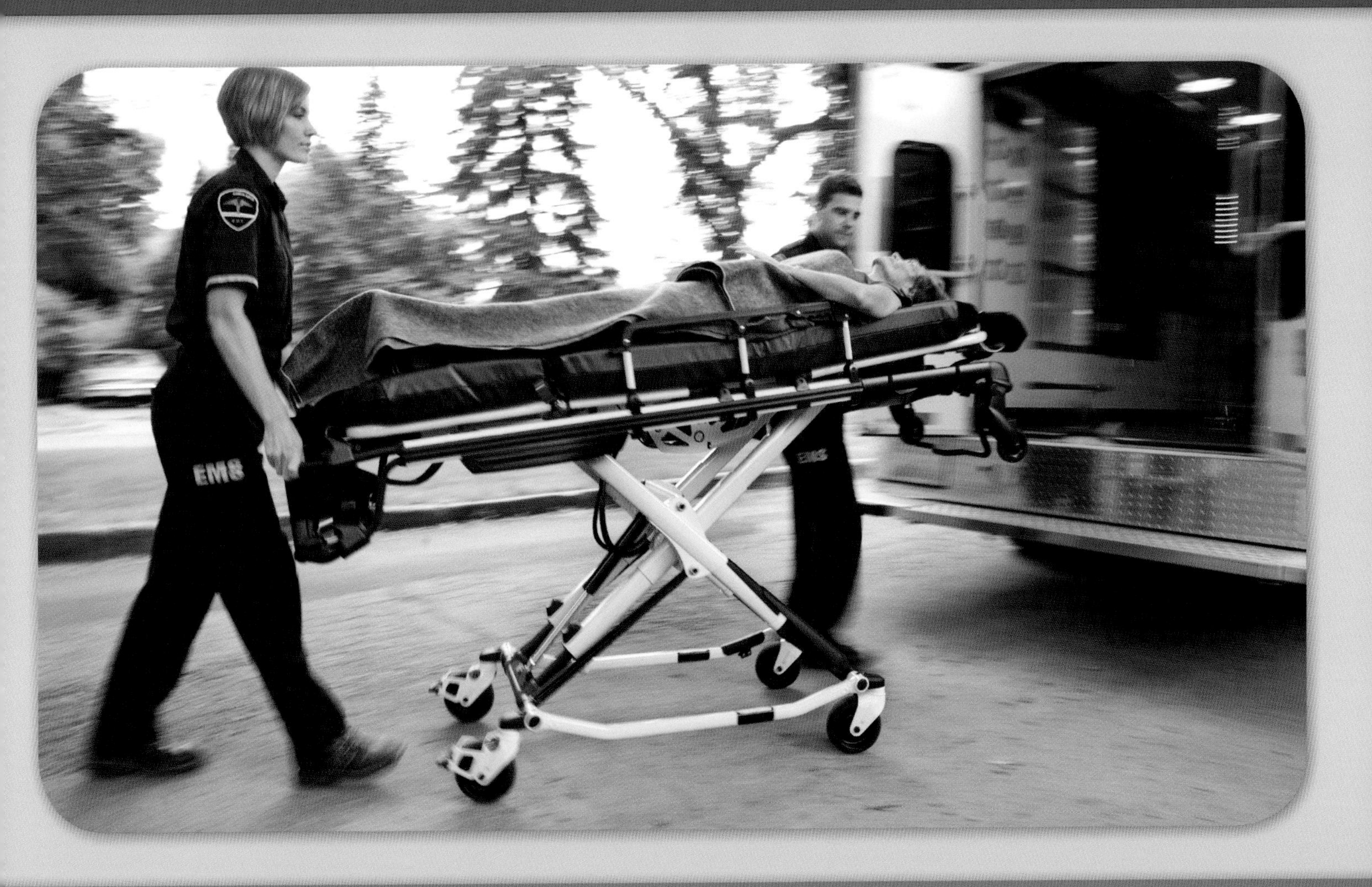

Paula and Jake move a patient to an ambulance. The gurney's wheels make it easy to move.

OXYGEN MASK

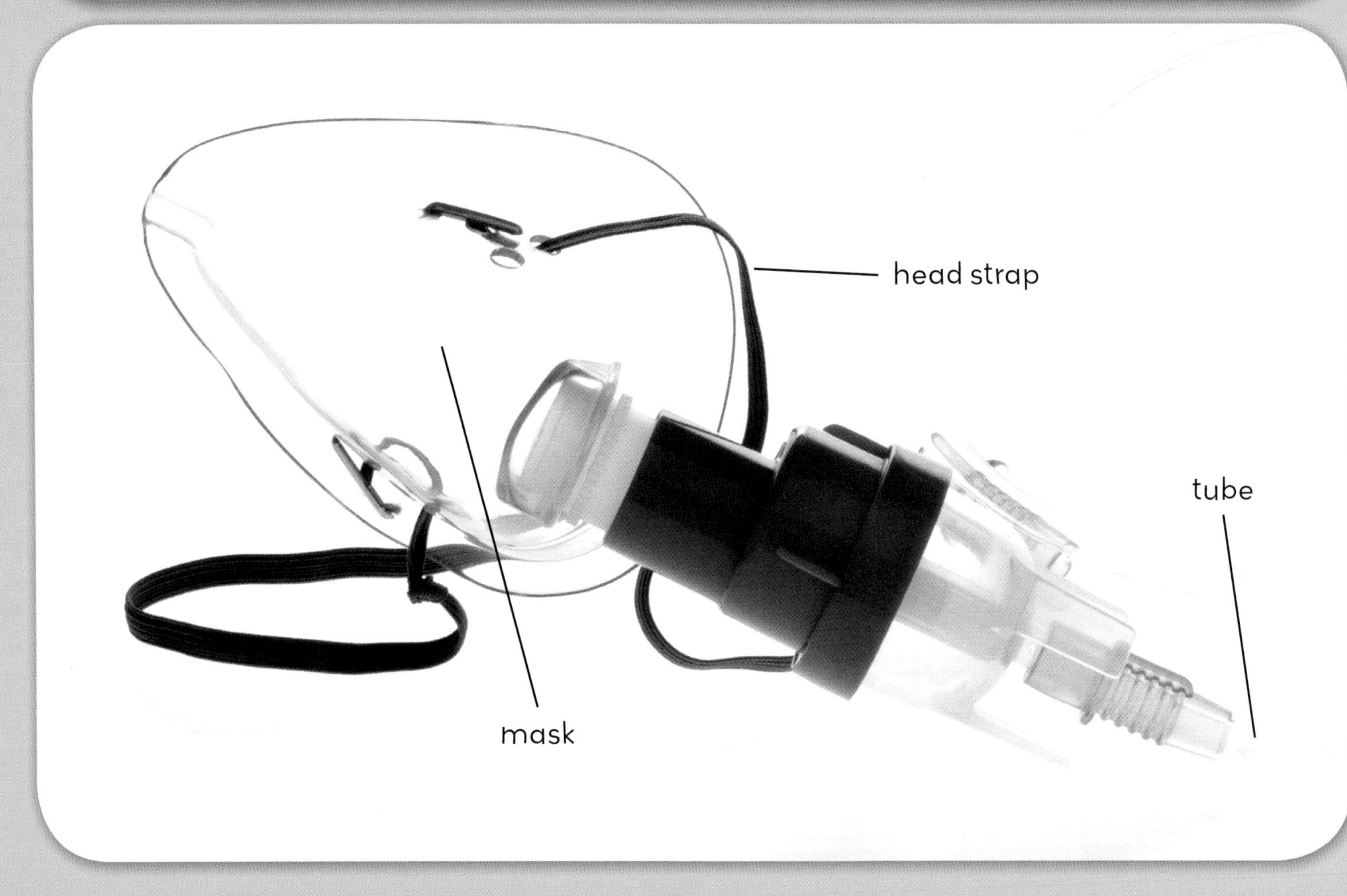

Oxygen masks allow patients to breathe more oxygen.

Everyone needs oxygen. It makes up about 21% of the air we breathe.

When someone is badly **injured**, his or her body needs more oxygen. Oxygen masks provide extra oxygen so patients can heal faster.

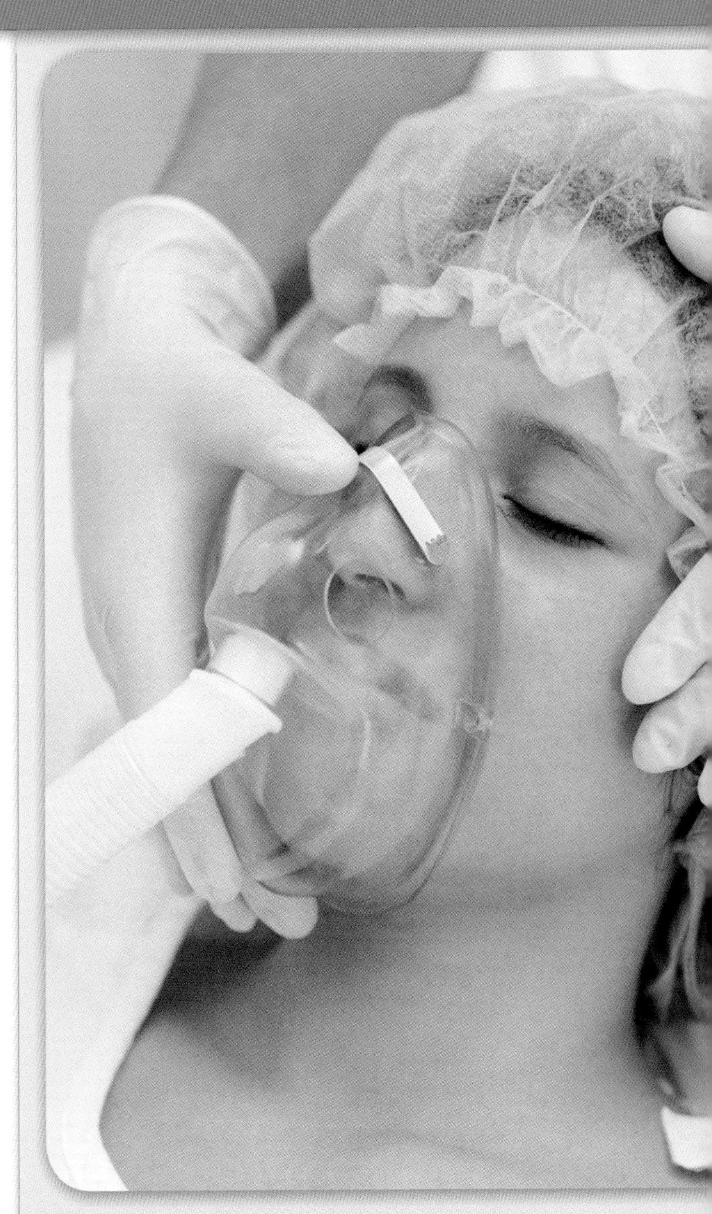

FAST FACT: EMTs can control the amount of oxygen a patient receives.

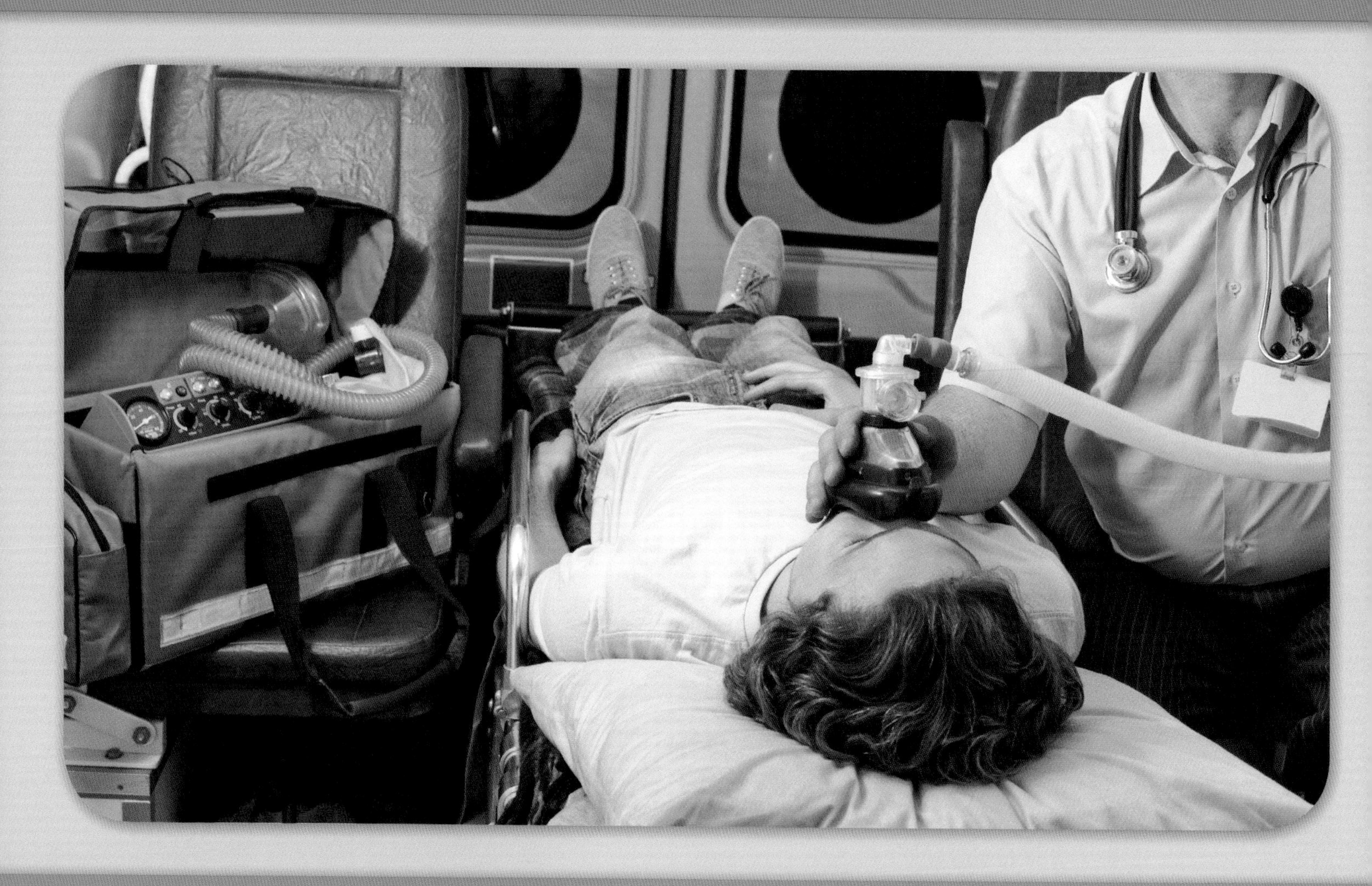

Greg is in shock. His body doesn't have enough oxygen. An oxygen mask gives him the extra oxygen he needs.

FAST FACT: Too much oxygen can be harmful to the body.

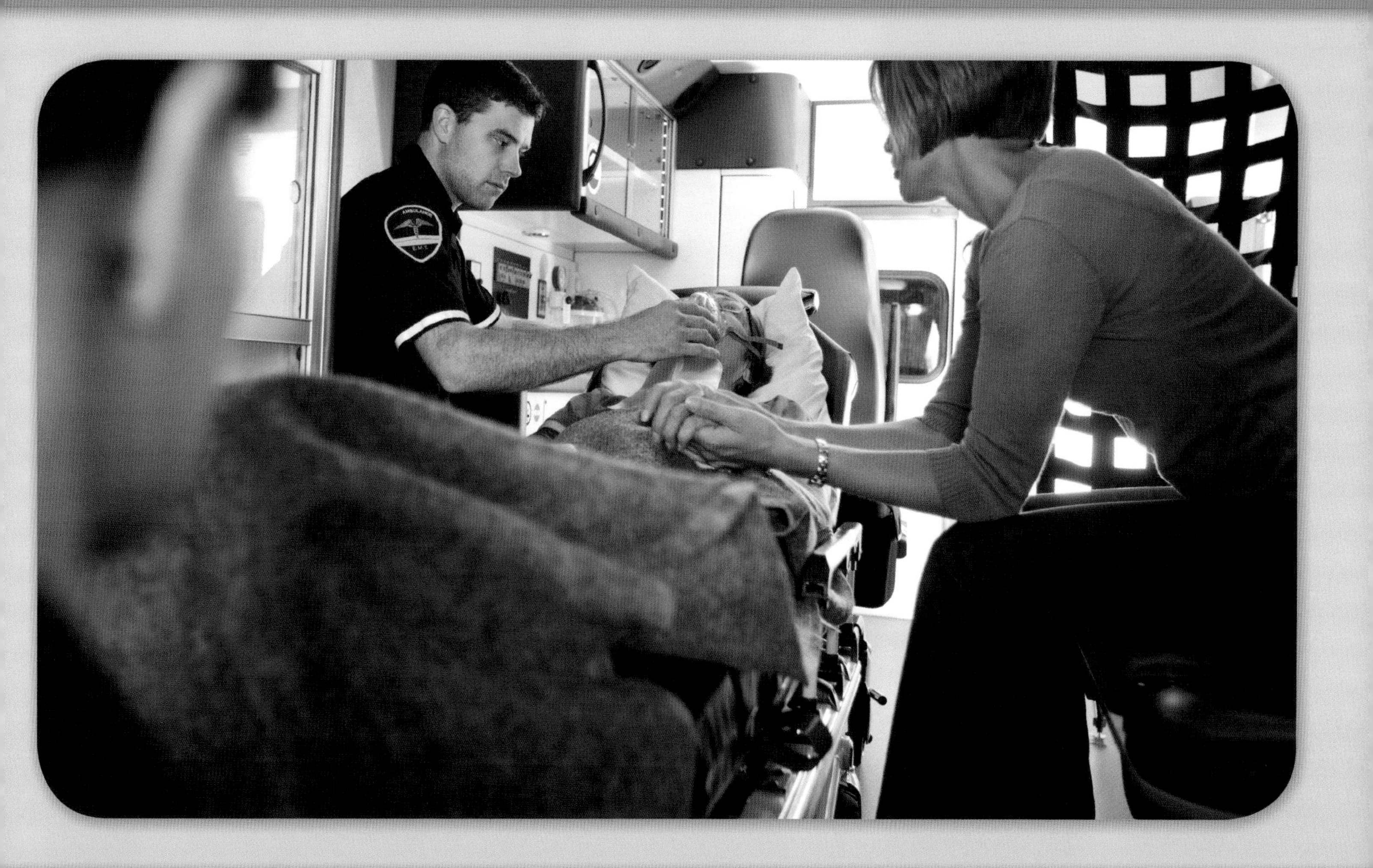

Carl is an EMT. He is treating a victim of a car accident. He helps her breathe through an oxygen mask.

MATCH GAME

MATCH THE WORDS TO THE PICTURES!

The answers are on the bottom of the page.

1. oxygen mask
2. ambulance
3. defibrillator
4. gurney

a. 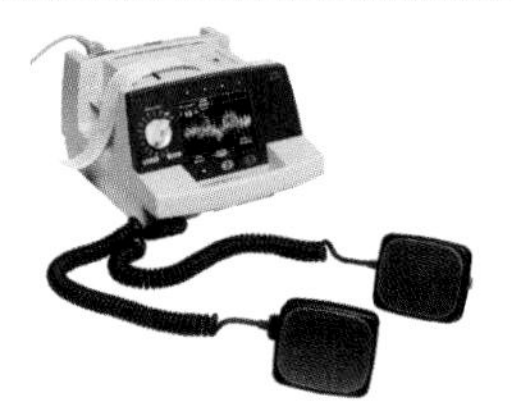

b. 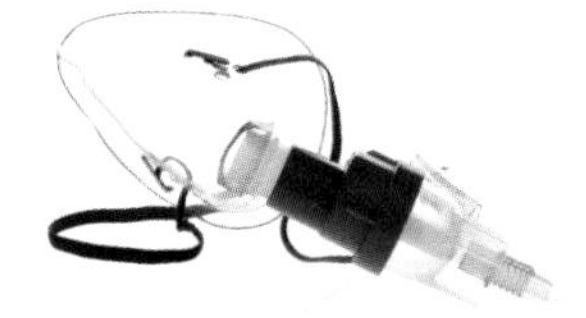

c. 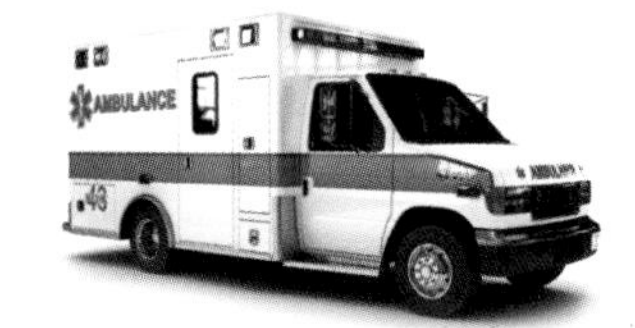

d. 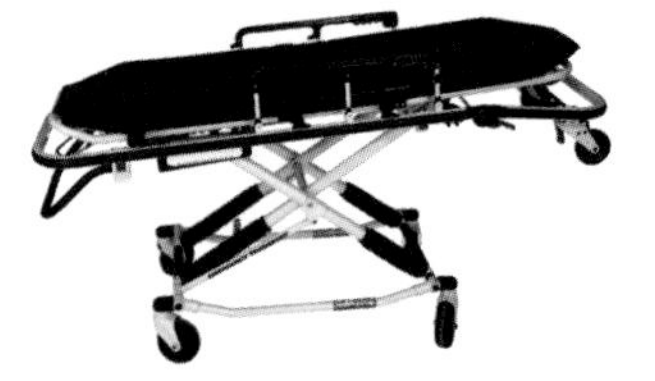

Answers: 1) b 2) c 3) a 4) d

TOOL QUIZ

TEST YOUR TOOL KNOWLEDGE!

The answers are on the bottom of the page.

1.

Ambulances allow EMTs to get to an accident quickly.

TRUE OR FALSE?

2.

Defibrillator paddles are placed on either side of the head.

TRUE OR FALSE?

3.

Gurneys have wheels.

TRUE OR FALSE?

4.

The air we breathe is 100% oxygen.

TRUE OR FALSE?

Answers: **1)** true **2)** false **3)** true **4)** false

GLOSSARY

battlefield – a place where a battle is fought.

emergency – a sudden, unexpected, dangerous situation that requires immediate attention.

equipment – a set of tools or items used for a special purpose or activity.

injured – hurt, wounded, or damaged.

medical – having to do with doctors or health.

modified – changed or altered to meet a certain need.

portable – easily moved or carried.

pulse – the beat or throb caused by the heart pumping blood through the body.

revive – to bring someone back to life.

siren – a device that makes a loud sound as a signal or warning.

stretcher – a flat board used to carry someone who is sick or hurt.

technician – a person who is skilled at a specific task.